The PROV
God's V

A Knit and Crochet Bible Study Personal Devotional and Journal

She shops around for the best yarns… and enjoys knitting and (crochet)…..

Prov 31:13 MSG

by TerryAnn Porter

Copyright Notices

© 2017, TerryAnn Porter

Copyright © 2017 by TerryAnn Porter   All rights reserved For personal use only . Abstracting with credit is permitted. To copy otherwise in any fashion physical or digital, to republish, to post on servers, or to redistribute to lists, requires prior specific permission and/or a fee. Request permissions from TerryAnn@KnittingBibleStudy.com

"Scripture taken from *The Message*. Copyright © 1993, 1994, 1995, 1996, 2000, 2001, 2002. Used by permission of NavPress Publishing Group."

THE HOLY BIBLE, NEW INTERNATIONAL VERSION®, NIV® Copyright © 1973, 1978, 1984, 2011 by Biblica, Inc.® Used by permission. All rights reserved worldwide.

Scripture quotations marked (NLT) are taken from the Holy Bible, New Living Translation, copyright © 1996, 2004, 2007 by Tyndale House Foundation. Used by permission of Tyndale House Publishers, Inc., Carol Stream, Illinois 60188. All rights reserved.

INTRODUCTION

Who is the Proverbs 31 woman? Some say she represents a perfection that can never be achieved. Others say she is a woman who has a full time corporate job and maintains perfectly her family and home as well.

Today's woman has many strings pulling on her. Society says she is of little value if she doesn't have a full time job. That she must also be mother of the year giving each child many hours of dutiful attention and be a sexy vixen at night for her husband. Society doesn't limit it to her husband, she's just to be a sexy vixen for any man.

Both designs of the woman seem illusive. What does God desire for a woman?

Within these pages you will take a look at Proverbs 31:10-31 and find out for yourself what a godly woman is and what a Proverbs 31 woman is. Can she really exist in today's world?

If you read the first verse of the 31st chapter of Proverbs you find a little tidbit of information that is often overlooked. These words are an oracle, a legacy, taught to him by his mother. Just like your mother told you what to look for in a man as you were growing up, Solomon's mother, Bathsheba, told him all these things to guide him in seeking a wife.

This woman is not born with all the qualities listed in the proverb. She grows into this woman. She learns how to be righteous and caring. She studies to become knowledgeable and creative.

Is there a woman in your life that you look upon as a "Proverbs 31 woman"? Her husband shows her respect, her children admire her, she bakes cookies for every event and attends each church function. She never speaks ill of anyone. Watching her you are certain she has a professional hairdresser under her bed because she always looks nice.

Ask her about her life and you will find out she learned how to treat her husband in a manner that in turn allowed him to treat her with such respect. It wasn't that way from the start of their marriage. She had to learn to cook for him, they had to learn how to communicate with each other. The qualities were there, they needed to be developed. Talk with her about her early days on her own, her newly married days, and you will be presented an entirely different person than the one before you today. She was knit into this person through trials, joys, mistakes and faith.

On each page we will take a look at the passage, using 4 different versions of Scripture. We will use the NIV, KJV, NLT and MSG. Different words with same meanings sometimes make it easier to understand. I am sure once we complete the study you will find that you are closer to being the Proverbs 31 woman than you think.

This book is different than the Kindle version in that you are given space to journal your thoughts.

Authors Note: I have used knit and crochet terms interchangeably throughout this book. Personally I enjoy both skills. Some enjoy one or the other and get upset at the mixed reference. I intend no disrespect or endorsement of one over the other.

STITCH ALONG:

Life is like a series of knit/crochet blocks, each sufficient on their own, but woven together they make a beautiful blanket. As a project in this study you might consider making a blanket by yourself or work with a friend, each of you preparing blocks to learn new stitches then seam them together.

As a project, consider the "Colors of Salvation" afghan pattern at the end of this book. If you would like a color version with pictures of this pattern go to the website www.KnitAndCrochetBibleStudy.com to download it.

As you grow in grace, stature, and faith you become like these blocks. At one time in your life you were a simple garter stitch or one of single crochet. Then you grew into the stockinette or double crochet. With school, work and family responsibilities the stitches changed, they twisted and turned; one day a chevron pattern, another day a basket weave.

Through each trial, struggle and accomplishment you become more stitched into the person you are today and the person you are becoming. God is still knitting away. You are a work in progress. God has not finished off and woven in the strings of your life yet. ☺

Table of Contents

- *Proverbs 31:10 You Are Valuable* 7
- *Proverbs 31:11,12 Can You Be Trusted?* 13
- *Proverbs 31:13, 14 Busy, Busy, Busy* 19
- *Proverbs 31:15, 17 Will Work For Food* 28
- *Proverbs 31:16, 18, 19 Plan Ahead* 34
- *Proverbs 31:20, 21, 22 Be Prepared* 41
- *Proverbs 31: 24 Knit to Sell* 48
- *Proverbs 31:25,26 Cat Got Your Tongue?* 54
- *Proverbs 31:27,28, 29 Priorities* 61
- *Proverbs 31:30, 31 Inner Beauty Outshines All* 68
- *Colors of Salvation Afghan* 75
- *ORANGE: GATES OF HELL* 82
- *WHITE: PURITY* 84
- *GOLD: HEAVEN* 87
- *BLUE: WATER OF BAPTISM* 89
- *GREEN: GROWING IN CHRIST* 91
- *PURPLE: ROYALTY* 94
- *FINISHING* 98
- *Afterword* 100

Proverbs 31:10 You Are Valuable

A wife of noble character who can find? She is worth far more than rubies. (NIV)

Who can find a virtuous woman? For her price is far above rubies. (KJV)

Who can find a virtuous and capable wife? She is worth more than precious rubies. (NLT)

A good woman is hard to find, and worth far more than diamonds. (MSG)

Just how valuable are you? God says you are His masterpiece, His most valuable creation. You are also created for a purpose according to *Ephesians 2:10.* You are created to do the good things he planned long ago. It sounds like a lot of pressure placed on our shoulders, but there is another part of that verse that we tend to forget. *"For we are God's masterpiece. He created us anew <u>in Christ Jesus,</u> so we can do the good things he planned for us long ago."*

Imagine I am holding a ball of yarn. By itself it may look nice, I could set it on the table and it might be decorative, but there is very little value from the ball of string. What if I start to knit/crochet a project with this yarn. Ah, now something usable is developing. As I work the pattern I will make mistakes. Each mistake affects the project. If I correct it, I learn a lesson and move on. If I ignore it the mistake may be unseen, like a sin hidden in my heart, or it may be obvious and add character to the project, just like life mistakes I have made add to the person I am today.

So how do we learn to become a woman of noble character, capable and valuable? Seek God's Word and learn from others who have achieved that status. *"Don't copy the behavior and customs of this world, but let God transform you into a new person by changing the way you think. Then you will learn to know God's will for you, which is good and pleasing and perfect."* (Rom 12:2 NLT)

Become like the ball of yarn, available to be knitted by God's hands into a virtuous woman of noble character. He will knit you into His eternal plan. When you mess up, He will guide you through the repair process and continue stitching as you become a valuable creation. For you are His most valuable work in progress.

Stitched in Prayer

- PATTERN VERSE: *Ephesians 2:10 "For we are God's masterpiece. He created us anew <u>in Christ Jesus,</u> so we can do the good things he planned for us long ago."*

- How are you progressing as a Proverbs 31 woman? What changes do you feel you would need to make in your life to become more like her?

- What will you do for yourself to become more "stitchable" by God?

PERSONAL JOURNAL   Today's date: _____

God, be with me during this quiet time. Calm my spirit, help me to focus on you and your love. Open my heart that I may hear you speak to me.

Scripture read today:

During my time with the Lord these people were brought to my mind and I pray for them:

Lord, you have made me mindful of these people. I pray your loving hand on them even if I don't know the situation. I do not need to know that Lord, I only need to follow your Word and pray for them.

For myself Lord I pray you will:

PRAISES

Lord, today I praise you for:

The woman to be admired and praised is the woman who lives in the Fear-of-God
                                            Prov. 31:30 *The* Message

    Praise the Lord. Praise God in his sanctuary; praise him in his mighty heavens. Praise him for his acts of power; praise him for his surpassing greatness. Praise him with the sounding of the trumpet, praise him with the harp and lyre, praise him with tambourine and dancing, praise him with the strings and flute, praise him with the clash of cymbals, praise him with resounding cymbals. Let everything that has breath praise the Lord.   Psalm 150

Proverbs 31:11,12 Can You Be Trusted?

Her husband has full confidence in her and lacks nothing of value. She brings him good, not harm, all the days of her life.   (NIV)

The heart of her husband doth safely trust in her, so that he shall have no need of spoil. She will do him good and not evil all the days of her life (KJV)

Her husband can trust her, and she will greatly enrich his life. She will not hinder him but help him all her life   (NLT)

Her husband trusts her without reserve, and never has reason to regret it.   Never spiteful, she treats him generously all her life long. (MSG)

If you are single your first inclination is probably to shun this part and discard its message. Please stay focused. There is more that can be learned about being the Proverbs 31 woman here.

The woman described here is trustworthy. Are you trustworthy? Does your husband know that what he tells you in confidence will not be discussed with your girlfriends, co-workers, or even in a bible study? How about your friends or family members, do they know that you will keep their confidences? Can you be trusted? If you divulge their secrets, put them down or speak badly of them to others, how can they trust you?

The Message version states she is "never spiteful".   Oh it is so easy sometimes when we've been wronged to wish something would happen to that person but that is not what we are called to do. *Romans 12:19* tells us *"do not take revenge my friends, but leave room for God's wrath.."* But God, it's not fair!! (I don't know if you do but, I say this so many times). The verse goes on though to rebuke and remind me *"for it is written: "It is mine to avenge; I will repay," says the Lord."*

When you are faced with difficulties at work there are co-workers watching to see how you respond. Many get their idea of what a Christian is by watching you. How are you representing God? Do you join in with group gossip? Or can you be trusted to mind your own business?

I love the way the Message reads in *Romans chapter 14, verses 8-11*. *"It's God we are answerable to - all the way from life to death and everything in between - not each other. That's why Jesus lived and died and then lived again: so that he could be our Master across the entire range of life and death, and free us from the petty tyrannies of each other. So where does that leave you when you criticize a brother? And where does that leave you when you condescend to a sister? I'd say it leaves you looking pretty silly - or worse. Eventually, we're all going to end up kneeling side by side in the place of judgment, facing God. Your critical and condescending ways aren't going to improve your position there one bit. Read it for yourself in Scripture: "As I live and breathe," God says, "every knee will bow before me; Every tongue will tell the honest truth that I and only I am God."* Then the knitting part comes in as verse 12 goes on. *"So tend to your knitting. You've got your hands full just taking care of your own life before God."*

Stitched in Prayer

- PATTERN VERSE: *Ephesians 5:1,2 "Be imitators of God and live a life of love, just as Christ loved us and gave himself up for us as a fragrant offering and sacrifice to God."*

- Would your family consider you to be trustworthy? What will you do to become more trustworthy in their eyes?

- It can become easy to slip into "tale telling" mode when others start telling stories about people around them. When tempted to add a little flavor to the conversation by adding something shared with you in confidence, silently recite *Romans 14:12 "So tend to your knitting (crochet). You've got your hands full just taking care of your own life before God."* Don't betray that confidence. You are answerable to God (*Romans 14:8*).

- What will you do this week to use your time more effectively than joining in the "tale telling" mode?

PERSONAL JOURNAL   Today's date: _____

God, be with me during this quiet time. Calm my spirit, help me to focus on you and your love. Open my heart that I may hear you speak to me.

Scripture read today:

During my time with the Lord these people were brought to my mind and I pray for them:

Lord, you have made me mindful of these people. I pray your loving hand on them even if I don't know the situation. I do not need to know that Lord, I only need to follow your Word and pray for them.

For myself Lord I pray you will:

PRAISES

Lord, today I praise you for:

The woman to be admired and praised is the woman who lives in the Fear-of-God
                                        Prov. 31:30 *The Message*

    Praise the Lord. Praise God in his sanctuary; praise him in his mighty heavens. Praise him for his acts of power; praise him for his surpassing greatness. Praise him with the sounding of the trumpet, praise him with the harp and lyre, praise him with tambourine and dancing, praise him with the strings and flute, praise him with the clash of cymbals, praise him with resounding cymbals. Let everything that has breath praise the Lord.   Psalm 150

Proverbs 31:13, 14 Busy, Busy, Busy

She selects wool and flax and works with eager hands. She is like the merchant ships, bringing her food from afar. (NIV)

She seeketh wool, and flax, and worketh willingly with her hands. She is like the merchants' ships; she bringeth her food from afar. (KJV)

She finds wool and flax and busily spins it. She is like a merchant's ship; she brings her food from afar. (NLT)

She shops around for the best yarns and cottons, and enjoys knitting and sewing. She's like a trading ship that sails to faraway places and brings back exotic surprises. (MSG)

I enjoy using 4 different versions here. When I looked at the words above I found *"she works with her hands; she seeks, finds and spins wool; she shops for the best materials; and she enjoys knitting and sewing."* Even if you don't knit or crochet, the Proverbs 31 woman is skillful. She cares for her home and she is creative not only in crafts but also in decorating her home and in food preparation for her family. This woman could put Martha Stewart to shame!!

The focus here is a heart attitude. She desires to make a comfortable home for her family. She clips coupons, seeks out sales, looks for ways to get a toddler to eat broccoli and begs her teenager to wear a scarf in cold weather even if the other kids don't have to wear one.

Proverbs 27:23 (MSG) says *"Know your sheep by name; carefully attend to your flocks...."* Put into the context of our study the sheep and flock are your family. *"Don't take them for granted"* it goes on to say, *"possessions don't last forever."* The children we are too busy to spend time with today will be out on their own too soon. *"You can knit sweaters from lambs' wool and sell your goats for a profit' There will be plenty of milk and meat to last your family through the winter."* Stay focused and check your heart attitude. Do you look at food preparation and knitting or crochet as an obligation or an opportunity?

Along with the full time job of running a home and maintaining a family, many women work another job outside the home. My favorite version was the Message which included *"she shops around for yarn and enjoys knitting"*. I find it easy sometimes to become so engulfed working on a knitted project that I forget to take care of other responsibilities. By the same token I also become so involved in work that I forget my bible reading and prayer life. I become so busy, I forget to start the evening meal or complete the load of laundry I started. How about you? Which obligation gets your best effort and most attention?

Sometimes we are just too busy. There is always something that needs to be done. *She works with eager hands,* but she is not to be so busy she forgets her family or her God.

God wants us to keep busy, but not so busy that we forget Him. Not even for a knitted project!!

Following is a prose I found several years ago. I cannot attribute the author as it appears to be unknown. The verse shows how easily we can become 'too busy'.

SATAN'S MEETING: (author unknown)

Satan called a worldwide convention of demons. In his opening address he said,
'We can't keep Christians from going to church.'
'We can't keep them from reading their Bibles and knowing the truth.'
'We can't even keep them from forming an intimate relationship with their Saviour.'
'Once they gain that connection with Jesus, our power over them is broken.'
'So let them go to their churches; let them have their covered dish dinners, BUT steal their time, so they don't have time to develop a relationship with Jesus Christ..'

'This is what I want you to do,' said the devil: 'Distract them from gaining hold of their Saviour and maintaining that vital connection throughout their day!'

'How shall we do this?' his demons shouted.

 'Keep them busy in the non-essentials of life and invent innumerable schemes to occupy their minds,' he answered.

'Tempt them to spend, spend, spend, and borrow, borrow, borrow.'
 'Persuade the wives to go to work for long hours and the husbands to work 6-7 days each week, 10-12 hours a day, so they can afford their empty lifestyles.'
 'Keep them from spending time with their children.'
 'As their families fragment, soon, their homes will offer no escape from the pressures of work!'   'Over-stimulate their minds so that they cannot hear that still, small voice.'
 'Entice them to play the radio or CD whenever they drive.' To keep the TV, DVDS, CDs and their PCs going constantly in their home and see to it that every store and restaurant in the world plays non-biblical music constantly.'
 'This will jam their minds and break that union with Christ.'

'Fill the coffee tables with magazines and newspapers.'
'Pound their minds with the news 24 hours a day.'
'Invade their driving moments with billboards.'
'Flood their mailboxes with junk mail, mail order catalogs, sweepstakes, and every kind of newsletter and promotional offering free products, services and false hopes..'
'Keep skinny, beautiful models on the magazines and TV so their husbands will believe that outward beauty is what's important, and they'll become dissatisfied with their wives. '
'Keep the wives too tired to love their husbands at night.'
'Give them headaches too! ' 'If they don't give their husbands the love they need, they will begin to look elsewhere.' 'That will fragment their families quickly!'

'Give them Santa Claus to distract them from teaching their children the real meaning of Christ.' 'Give them an Easter bunny so they won't talk about his resurrection and power over sin and death.'

'Even in their recreation, let them be excessive.' 'Have them return from their recreation exhausted.' 'Keep them too busy to go out in nature and reflect on God's creation. Send them to amusement parks, sporting events, plays, concerts, and movies instead.'
'Keep them busy, busy, busy!'

'And when they meet for spiritual fellowship, involve them in gossip and small talk so that they leave with troubled consciences.' 'Crowd their lives with so many good causes they have no time to seek power from Jesus.' 'Soon they will be working in their own strength, sacrificing their health and family for the good of the cause.'

'It will work!'
'It will work!'

It was quite a plan!   The demons went eagerly to their assignments causing Christians everywhere to get busier and more rushed, going here and there.   Having little time for their God or their families. Having no time to tell others about the power of Jesus to change lives.

I guess the question is, has the devil been successful in his schemes?

You be the judge!!!!!

author unknown

Stitched in Prayer

- PATTERN VERSE: *Psalm 46:10, "Be still and know that I am God".*

- Are you "too busy"? Consider keeping a journal of all your activities through the week. What obligation is getting your most attention and best efforts?

- How will you more effectively use your time this week?

PERSONAL JOURNAL   Today's date: _____

God, be with me during this quiet time. Calm my spirit, help me to focus on you and your love. Open my heart that I may hear you speak to me.

Scripture read today:

During my time with the Lord these people were brought to my mind and I pray for them:

Lord, you have made me mindful of these people. I pray your loving hand on them even if I don't know the situation. I do not need to know that Lord, I only need to follow your Word and pray for them.

For myself Lord I pray you will:

PRAISES

Lord, today I praise you for:

The woman to be admired and praised is the woman who lives in the Fear-of-God
                                    Prov. 31:30 The Message

Praise the Lord. Praise God in his sanctuary; praise him in his mighty heavens. Praise him for his acts of power; praise him for his surpassing greatness. Praise him with the sounding of the trumpet, praise him with the harp and lyre, praise him with tambourine and dancing, praise him with the strings and flute, praise him with the clash of cymbals, praise him with resounding cymbals. Let everything that has breath praise the Lord.   Psalm 150

Proverbs 31:15, 17 Will Work For Food

She gets up while it is still dark; she provides food for her family and portions for her servant girls She sets about her work vigorously; her arms are strong for her tasks. . (NIV)

She riseth also while it is yet night, and giveth meat to her household, and a portion to her maidens. She girdeth her loins with strength, and strengthens her arms. KJV)

She gets up before dawn to prepare breakfast for her household and plan the day's work for her servant girls. She is energetic and strong, a hard worker. (NLT)

She's up before dawn, preparing breakfast for her family and organizing her day First thing in the morning, she dresses for work, rolls up her sleeves, eager to get started. . (MSG)

There is an old adage that goes "a man works from sun to sun but a women's work is never done". It always seems there is more to do, even when you think you've completed it all. Lately I've been feeling there is more on my TO DO list than my GOT IT DONE list. Can you relate?

These scriptures remind us that while she is busy and working she also delegates. Look at the NLT version *"and plans the day's work for her servant girls"*. I don't happen to have any servant girls and don't know anyone who does, but I can delegate in other ways. I can hire someone to do the yard work so I can keep up with the inside work. I can make up a list of things to be done and post them so my family can also complete some chores. What ideas would you add?

Notice the MSG uses the words *"she organizes her day"*. She plans things out so she can stay on top of them. Many women today use daily planners, do you have one? There are many appointments that fill the calendar. If there is an appointment, we tend to make all necessary arrangements to be there. When they were younger my daughters joked that they knew once I said "I have you on my Outlook calendar" it was set in stone and our interaction would definitely occur. Do you have an appointment with God on your calendar? He wants to spend some 'one on one' time with you.

The part that caught and held my attention, however, was in the MSG translation which reads she is *"eager to get started"*. How eager are you first thing in the morning? For myself, I try to hide under the covers and pretend morning hasn't arrived. Do you jump out of bed, throw on your clothes and rush to work? Eagerly? Do you start your day with a prayer? Confidently?

As busy as we are, it is important too, to take time to rest. Remember that after creating the earth, the skies and seas, plants and animals, and man and woman, *God rested from all his work* (*Genesis 2:2*). While you work with strength and vigor, you must also commit yourself to living healthy. That means rest, sleep, a balanced diet, maintaining appropriate weight and strong muscles. Oh my gosh, now you added more to my list of things to do !?!?! *Psalm 90:12* reads *"teach us to make the most of our time, so that we may grow in wisdom."* We have much to do, God doesn't want us to do it alone. He wants us to eagerly approach each day, spend time with him, knit/crochet a little, and care for the family He has given us. *Job 7:6* in the MESSAGE explains this pattern well. *"My days come and go swifter than the click of knitting needles, and then the yarn runs out—an unfinished life!"*

Be a wise manager of what you've got; including your time. We must work, whether it is solely being a homemaker, or a homemaker and corporate worker. But don't become weary. You don't have to do it alone In *Matthew 11:29* Jesus offers *"come to me all who are weary and heavy-laden, and I will give you rest."* After your work, pick up your yarn, relax, and talk to God.

Stitched in Prayer

- **PATTERN VERSE:** *Proverbs 31:17 First thing in the morning, she dresses for work, rolls up her sleeves, eager to get started.*

- How do you prepare for each new day?

- How do you glorify God in your daily activities? What changes will you make to be ready for the day?

- How are you ensuring you get enough rest from the day's work?

PERSONAL JOURNAL   Today's date: _____

God, be with me during this quiet time. Calm my spirit, help me to focus on you and your love. Open my heart that I may hear you speak to me.

Scripture read today:

During my time with the Lord these people were brought to my mind and I pray for them:

Lord, you have made me mindful of these people. I pray your loving hand on them even if I don't know the situation. I do not need to know that Lord, I only need to follow your Word and pray for them.

For myself Lord I pray you will:

PRAISES

Lord, today I praise you for:

The woman to be admired and praised is the woman who lives in the Fear-of-God
                              Prov. 31:30 The Message

Praise the Lord. Praise God in his sanctuary; praise him in his mighty heavens. Praise him for his acts of power; praise him for his surpassing greatness. Praise him with the sounding of the trumpet, praise him with the harp and lyre, praise him with tambourine and dancing, praise him with the strings and flute, praise him with the clash of cymbals, praise him with resounding cymbals. Let everything that has breath praise the Lord.   Psalm 150

Proverbs 31:16, 18, 19   Plan Ahead

She considers a field and buys it; out of her earnings she plants a vineyard. She sees that her trading is profitable, and her lamp does not go out at night. In her hand she holds the distaff and grasps the spindle with her fingers. (NIV)

She considereth a field, and buyeth it; with the fruit of her hands she planteth a vineyard. She perceiveth that her merchandise is good; her candle goeth not out by night She layeth her hands to the spindle, and her hands hold the distaff. (KJV)

She goes out to inspect a field and buys it; with her earnings she plants a vineyard. She watches for bargains; her lights burn late into the night. Her hands are busy spinning thread, her fingers twisting fiber. (NLT)

She looks over a field and buys it, then, with money she's put aside, plants a garden. She senses the worth of her work, is in no hurry to call it quits for the day. She's skilled in the crafts of home and hearth, diligent in homemaking. ((MSG)

You don't have to run your own business or be the CEO of a large corporation to accomplish what is described in these verses. This woman is an entrepreneur managing a home and family. She plans for the future seeking ways to improve on what she has and to meet her family needs. She sets goals and is a good steward of time and money.

God wants us to take care of what He has given us. *"From everyone who has been given much, much will be demanded; and from the one who has been entrusted with much, much more will be asked".* (Luke 12:48 NIV). Some women don't have as much as others. But each is responsible for what she has. *"She watches for bargains, her hands are busy, she's diligent in homemaking".*

According to dictionary dot com, a distaff is <u>a staff with a cleft end for holding wool, flax, etc., from which the thread is drawn in spinning by hand</u>. To spin you must draw out the fibers and add twists until you create a stable yarn. Pulling and twisting continues throughout the process. Isn't life like that? Full of twists and tugs when you need to push and pull yourself through problems and issues.

She becomes skilled in handling these situations and is busy spinning threads of patience and twisting fibers of love into her home. Does she do all this immediately and without training and practice? NO!!! Remember when you learned how to knit or crochet? Did you pick up yarn and make a sweater? No, you first learned how to hold the hook or needle and yarn, you learned basic then more advanced stitches, you learned how to end your project and even to sew seams. It took time. Even if you were a fast learner this was not accomplished in the first few hours of learning.

Once you leave your parent's home and begin to run your own home you won't have all the talents your mother did when you left. You need to develop them, just as she did. Don't be hard on yourself if you are not accomplished at everything. Take time to learn how to manage your home and family. Some will adjust quickly, others will take longer. Both can become a Proverbs 31 woman.

She plans ahead. She sees the field and plants a vineyard. She sees what that field can provide with planning and work. When you pick up your yarn you plan out what it will be and work toward that end.

Look at what God has offered you. Prayerfully consider what will become of your vineyard.

Stitched in Prayer

- **VERSE OF THE WEEK:** *1 Corinthians 13:11. "When I was a child, I talked like a child. I thought like a child. I reasoned like a child. When I became a woman I put childish ways behind me."*

- How will you improve the stewardship of your home and family?

- What will you do to become more responsible with what God has given you?

- How do you see yourself in 1 year? In 5 years? In 10 years? Are you drawing closer to God?

PERSONAL JOURNAL   Today's date: _____

God, be with me during this quiet time. Calm my spirit, help me to focus on you and your love. Open my heart that I may hear you speak to me.

Scripture read today:

During my time with the Lord these people were brought to my mind and I pray for them:

Lord, you have made me mindful of these people. I pray your loving hand on them even if I don't know the situation. I do not need to know that Lord, I only need to follow your Word and pray for them.

For myself Lord I pray you will:

PRAISES

Lord, today I praise you for:

The woman to be admired and praised is the woman who lives in the Fear-of-God
                                        Prov. 31:30 The Message

Praise the Lord. Praise God in his sanctuary; praise him in his mighty heavens. Praise him for his acts of power; praise him for his surpassing greatness. Praise him with the sounding of the trumpet, praise him with the harp and lyre, praise him with tambourine and dancing, praise him with the strings and flute, praise him with the clash of cymbals, praise him with resounding cymbals. Let everything that has breath praise the Lord.   Psalm 150

Proverbs 31:20, 21, 22   Be Prepared

She opens her arms to the poor and extends her hands to the needy. When it snows, she has no fear for her household; for all of them are clothed in scarlet. She makes coverings for her bed; she is clothed in fine linen and purple.   (NIV)

She stretches out her hand to the poor; yea, she reacheth forth her hands to the needy She is not afraid of the snow for her household; for all her household are clothed with scarlet. She maketh herself coverings of tapestry; her clothing is silk and purple.   (KJV)

She extends a helping hand to the poor and opens her arms to the needy She has no fear of winter for her household because all of them have warm clothes. She quilts her own bedspreads. She dresses like royalty in gowns of finest cloth.   (NLT)

She's quick to assist anyone in need, reaches out to the poor. She doesn't worry about her family when it snows; their winter clothes are all mended and ready to wear. She makes her own clothing, and dresses in colorful linens and silks (MSG)

Is there anything this woman can't do? Now she is helping the needy, making her clothing and bedspreads and dressing to the nines. And she does it without worry or fear !!!

I have a plaque in my home that reads "Worry does not empty tomorrow of its troubles. It empties today of is strength" and another "Why worry when you can pray". I need the reminders because I find it easier to worry than to pray because when I worry, I am the focus. It is hard to let go. I am in charge and I don't trust anyone else, including God, to handle the situation. Unfortunately I have learned that my worry does not fix anything. No, not one problem has been solved by my worry. However, with worry more problems have occurred and I have done harm to my health and self esteem. God knows this. In Proverbs 12:25 we are told *"worry weighs us down."* When I am involved in worry it is like standing in a field of mud, I tire just trying to lift my leg to move forward and then I just sink deeper to struggle again to move forward. I cannot think clearly and I cannot make sound decisions. Does that sound familiar? Do you experience the same?

When I pray and seek God, the focus is removed from myself and I am able to see the needs of others. I can make clear decisions. I may not be able to make a bedspread but I can take unused blankets from my closet and offer them to a shelter. I can offer household items from the closet that I never use to the Salvation Army or Goodwill so others may benefit from them. I can take the time once or twice a month to help serve food at a soup kitchen. I can knit hats and sweaters for local charities or missions.

If I allow God to direct me and prayerfully seek His guidance I can be prepared for life's unexpected burdens and the harshness of winter. Note the Proverbs 31 women has *"no fear for her household'*. Her full confidence is in the Lord and because of that she is prepared to guide her family through difficult times.

There is a story in *Matthew 25* comparing 5 virgins who are prepared for the unknown time of return of the bridegroom and 5 who are not prepared. Let's read the passage.

"At that time the kingdom of heaven will be like ten virgins who took their lamps and went out to meet the bridegroom. Five of them were foolish and five were wise. The foolish ones took their lamps but did not take any oil with them. The wise, however, took oil in jars along with their lamps. The bridegroom was a long time in coming, and they all became drowsy and fell asleep.

"At midnight the cry rang out: 'Here's the bridegroom! Come out to meet him!' "Then all the virgins woke up and trimmed their lamps. The foolish ones said to the wise, 'Give us some of your oil; our lamps are going out.' " 'No,' they replied, 'there may not be enough for both us and you. Instead, go to those who sell oil and buy some for yourselves.' "But while they were on their way to buy the oil, the bridegroom arrived. The virgins who were ready went in with him to

the wedding banquet. And the door was shut. "Later the others also came. 'Sir! Sir!' they said. 'Open the door for us!' "But he replied, 'I tell you the truth, I don't know you.' "Therefore keep watch, because you do not know the day or the hour." Matt 25:1-13 (NIV)

Two lessons come from this story (1) be prepared and (2) it's OK to say NO and not give up your family necessities. You are not responsible for choices made by others.

This woman has much to do and is prepared to serve her family using whatever she has, including her skills.

A knitting or crochet pattern instructs each step of the process to make the desired item. Before starting, you are encouraged to read the pattern through so that you are aware of what is coming up in the pattern and to allow you to be prepared for various twists and turns in the pattern. Many projects have been frogged (rip-it, rip-it, rip-it) because the words "at the same time" or "change needle/hook size" were missed while stitching.

Along the way in life there are bumps in the road and unexpected problems. If we look to God and keep walking with Him He will keep us prepared to help others and provide for our families.

Stitched in Prayer

- **PATTERN VERSE:** *Proverbs 12:25*
  "Worry weighs us down"

- How has worry helped you?

- How do you determine priorities in your life and how do you know when to say 'no' to others without worrying?

- No one knows the day Christ will return. How are you prepared for His return?

PERSONAL JOURNAL   Today's date: _____

God, be with me during this quiet time. Calm my spirit, help me to focus on you and your love. Open my heart that I may hear you speak to me.

Scripture read today:

During my time with the Lord these people were brought to my mind and I pray for them:

Lord, you have made me mindful of these people. I pray your loving hand on them even if I don't know the situation. I do not need to know that Lord, I only need to follow your Word and pray for them.

For myself Lord I pray you will:

PRAISES

Lord, today I praise you for:

The woman to be admired and praised is the woman who lives in the Fear-of-God
                                         Prov. 31:30 The Message

Praise the Lord. Praise God in his sanctuary; praise him in his mighty heavens. Praise him for his acts of power; praise him for his surpassing greatness. Praise him with the sounding of the trumpet, praise him with the harp and lyre, praise him with tambourine and dancing, praise him with the strings and flute, praise him with the clash of cymbals, praise him with resounding cymbals. Let everything that has breath praise the Lord.   Psalm 150

Proverbs 31: 24   Knit to Sell

She makes linen garments and sells them, and supplies the merchants with sashes.   (NIV)

She maketh fine linen, and selleth it; and delivereth girdles unto the merchant.   (KJV)

She makes belted linen garments and sashes to sell to the merchants.   (NLT)

She designs gowns and sells them, brings the sweaters she knits to the dress shops.   (MSG)

God has provided each of us with talents and expects us to use them. You may not be able to make garments well enough to sell, but you have the ability to seek out bargains for your home. You may not have the ability to knit or crochet sweaters for dress shops but you may be able to work at a local store to add to your family finances.

All time and money you have are gifts from God. *"Remember the LORD your God, for it is he who gives you the ability to produce wealth." "You will be wealthy and your good deeds will last forever." "Honor God with everything you own." (Deut 8:19NIV; Ps 112:3NLT)*

It doesn't matter if you work outside the home or are a full time home maker. It doesn't matter if your job is an entry level position or the CEO of a large corporation. Even when you are busy mopping your kitchen floor or making your latest scarf, *"whatever you do, do heartily as unto the Lord" (see Col 3:23-24)*.

These things must be done with a pure heart, a heart seeking to please the Lord. A worker who is constantly grumbling, criticizing the boss and co-workers brings about discord. *"These people are grumblers and complainers, living only to satisfy their desires. They brag loudly about themselves, and they flatter others to get what they want." (Jude 1:16 NLT).* It can be hard not to be drawn into these actions. *"Therefore, prepare you minds for action; be self-controlled; set your hope fully on the grace to be given you when Jesus Christ is revealed. (1 Peter 1:13 NIV)*

Is the hard work and effort really worth it? *"We continually remember before our God and Father your work produced by faith, your labor prompted by love, and your endurance inspired by hope in our Lord Jesus Christ. (1 Thes 1:3 NIV).* Others around you may have heard you attend church and watch to see how you react in difficult situations. Neighbors watch as you work and play. When you knit/crochet and pass along your finished products you are silently witnessing.

Read the story of Esther. Orphaned at a young age she was raised by her uncle, then taken to be presented to the King as a candidate for Queen. She took to heart all she had been taught about honoring God. She showed grace in a difficult situation. She didn't design gowns or sell dresses to local shops, but she worked hard following the direction of Hegai and was taken by Xerxes to be his wife and Queen. She continued to honor God in the way she approached the King and sought to save the Israelites from being exterminated by Haman.

We all have talents to use for God's glory whether it be running a corporation, running a household, or stitching a sweater. How are you using these gifts?

Stitched in Prayer

- **PATTERN VERSE:** *Colossians 3:23 "whatever you do, do heartily as unto the Lord"*

- Have you been working and doing all things to please the Lord? How will you change your focus from pleasing man to pleasing the Lord?

- What will you do to more effectively use your knitting/crochet time to please the Lord?

PERSONAL JOURNAL   Today's date: _____

God, be with me during this quiet time. Calm my spirit, help me to focus on you and your love. Open my heart that I may hear you speak to me.

Scripture read today:

During my time with the Lord these people were brought to my mind and I pray for them:

Lord, you have made me mindful of these people. I pray your loving hand on them even if I don't know the situation. I do not need to know that Lord, I only need to follow your Word and pray for them.

For myself Lord I pray you will:

PRAISES

Lord, today I praise you for:

The woman to be admired and praised is the woman who lives in the Fear-of-God
                                    Prov. 31:30 *The Message*

Praise the Lord. Praise God in his sanctuary; praise him in his mighty heavens. Praise him for his acts of power; praise him for his surpassing greatness. Praise him with the sounding of the trumpet, praise him with the harp and lyre, praise him with tambourine and dancing, praise him with the strings and flute, praise him with the clash of cymbals, praise him with resounding cymbals. Let everything that has breath praise the Lord.   Psalm 150

Proverbs 31:25,26 Cat Got Your Tongue?

She is clothed with strength and dignity; she can laugh at the days to come. She speaks with wisdom, and faithful instruction is on her tongue. (NIV)

Strength and honour are her clothing; and she shall rejoice in time to come. She openeth her mouth with wisdom; and in her tongue is the law of kindness. (KJV)

She is clothed with strength and dignity, and she laughs with no fear of the future. When she speaks, her words are wise, and kindness is the rule when she gives instructions (NLT)

Her clothes are well-made and elegant, and she always faces tomorrow with a smile. When she speaks she has something worthwhile to say, and she always says it kindly (MSG)

The Proverbs 31 woman is pleased to be growing older, knowing that older doesn't necessarily mean weaker. Her inner strength and honor comes from a fellowship with Christ. Her confidence in the Lord gives her hope as she looks forward to the future. She speaks with a wisdom drawn from God's Word.

When you read these words is there a particular woman you know that comes to mind? For me it is a woman named Birdie. Though she is now at home with the Lord her time on earth was spent glorifying God. Whenever I was in her presence I felt the hand of God holding me close. She exuded His love and demonstrated it in every area of her life. You never left her presence without a prayer and word of encouragement. Even on her deathbed she asked after others with a genuine concern. She didn't fear her earthly future as she battled against the cancer that ravaged her body because she knew where her eternal home was.

Birdie demonstrated *Titus 2:7,8 "show them all this by doing it yourself, incorruptible in your teaching, your words solid and sane."* As we develop the qualities of the Proverbs 31 woman we are also required to model it. *"So don't lose a minute in building on what you've been given, complementing your basic faith with good character" (2 Peter 1:5)* Work hard to sow seeds of godly wisdom, encouragement, and truth with noble dignity.

Why do we need to demonstrate this love Christ has for us and offer words of encouragement with grace, dignity and strength? Perhaps *Colossians 2:2* can sum it up best. *"I want them to be encouraged and knit together by strong ties of love. I want them to have complete confidence that they understand God's mysterious plan, which is Christ himself."*

Look to Jesus Christ and seek the strength and confidence He desires to stitch within you.

Stitched in Prayer

- **PATTERN VERSE:** *Colossians 2:2 "I want them to be encouraged and knit together by strong ties of love. I want them to have complete confidence that they understand God's mysterious plan, which is Christ himself."*

- As you have been studying the Proverbs 31 woman what have you learned about your life? Journal what you have learned and what you are doing to become more like the godly woman described in these verses?

- Who in your life would you consider a true "Proverbs 31 woman"? Why?

- What will you do this week to encourage someone?

PERSONAL JOURNAL   Today's date: _____

God, be with me during this quiet time. Calm my spirit, help me to focus on you and your love. Open my heart that I may hear you speak to me.

Scripture read today:

During my time with the Lord these people were brought to my mind and I pray for them:

Lord, you have made me mindful of these people. I pray your loving hand on them even if I don't know the situation. I do not need to know that Lord, I only need to follow your Word and pray for them.

For myself Lord I pray you will:

PRAISES

Lord, today I praise you for:

The woman to be admired and praised is the woman who lives in the Fear-of-God
           Prov. 31:30 *The* Message

Praise the Lord. Praise God in his sanctuary; praise him in his mighty heavens. Praise him for his acts of power; praise him for his surpassing greatness. Praise him with the sounding of the trumpet, praise him with the harp and lyre, praise him with tambourine and dancing, praise him with the strings and flute, praise him with the clash of cymbals, praise him with resounding cymbals. Let everything that has breath praise the Lord.   Psalm 150

Proverbs 31:27,28, 29   Priorities

She watches over the affairs of her household and does not eat the bread of idleness. Her children arise and call her blessed; her husband also, and he praises her: "Many women do noble things, but you surpass them all"   (NIV)

She looketh well to the ways of her household, and eateth not the bread of idleness. Her children arise up, and call her blessed; her husband also, and he praiseth her. Many daughters have done virtuously, but thou excellest them all. (KJV)

She carefully watches all that goes on in her household and does not have to bear the consequences of laziness. Her children stand and bless her. Her husband praises her. "There are many virtuous and capable women in the world, but you surpass them all!" (NLT)

She keeps an eye on everyone in her household, and keeps them all busy and productive Her children respect and bless her; her husband joins in with words of praise; "Many women have done wonderful things, but you've outclassed them all!" (MSG)

We strive to make a pleasant home for our families and make every effort to keep everyone happy. It takes a lot of hard work, and to accomplish this a wise woman will order her priorities. She must create a healthy balance between work, knitting, crochet, playing, home care, and personal time with each family member.

Disciplining children can be frustrating but is necessary so they will grow up with manners, work ethics, and a love for the Lord. *"Fix these words of mine in your hearts and minds; tie them as symbols on your hands and bind them on your foreheads. Teach them to your children, talking about them when you sit at home and when you talk along the road, when you lie down and when you get up. (Deut 11:18.19).* God hears when we pray for our children. *"Lift up your hands to him in prayer, pleading for your children" (Lamentations 2:19).* Just as you discipline your child, God will discipline you. *(Proverbs 3:12) "He corrects those He loves"*. So get rid of the mommy guilt and continue to guide them. *Matthew 25:40* tells us *"I tell you the truth, whatever you did for one of the least of these, you did for me"*. The "least of these" includes caring for your children. Remember, as much as you love your children God loves them more.

This must be balanced with getting along with a spouse. Our husbands know the best and the worst of us. Keep him lifted in prayer. Talk to God about the strains and difficulties, listen for His still small voice to guide you in your marriage. If you don't take these things to God, don't take them to your friends.

Then the balance is upset further with the addition of work, children's various activities, church services, knitting/crochet meetings.. She watches over her home. She is certainly not lazy.

You may never hear words of praise from your children or husband but that doesn't mean your job is in vain. You don't have to handle these responsibilities alone. Just like you have a pattern to follow when you wish to make a blanket or sweater, within you is the light to guide others. *"We now have this light shining in our hearts, but we ourselves are like fragile clay jars containing this great treasure. This makes it clear that our great power is from God, not from ourselves."* *2 Corinthians 4:7 NLT* You are strong, your strength is from the Lord.

Stitched in Prayer

- PATTERN VERSE: *2 Corinthians 4:7 "We now have this light shining in our hearts, but we ourselves are like fragile clay jars containing this great treasure. This makes it clear that our great power is from God, not from ourselves."*

- With so much to do, how do you prioritize?

- Family members don't always say the words of praise we desire to hear. Look closely, in what other ways is your family showing their appreciation?

- How will you make honoring God a priority in your life?

PERSONAL JOURNAL   Today's date: _____

God, be with me during this quiet time. Calm my spirit, help me to focus on you and your love. Open my heart that I may hear you speak to me.

Scripture read today:

During my time with the Lord these people were brought to my mind and I pray for them:

Lord, you have made me mindful of these people. I pray your loving hand on them even if I don't know the situation. I do not need to know that Lord, I only need to follow your Word and pray for them.

For myself Lord I pray you will:

PRAISES

Lord, today I praise you for:

The woman to be admired and praised is the woman who lives in the Fear-of-God
                                        Prov. 31:30 The Message

Praise the Lord. Praise God in his sanctuary; praise him in his mighty heavens. Praise him for his acts of power; praise him for his surpassing greatness. Praise him with the sounding of the trumpet, praise him with the harp and lyre, praise him with tambourine and dancing, praise him with the strings and flute, praise him with the clash of cymbals, praise him with resounding cymbals. Let everything that has breath praise the Lord.   Psalm 150

Proverbs 31:30, 31   Inner Beauty Outshines All

Charm is deceptive, and beauty is fleeting; but a woman who fears the Lord is to be praised. Give her the reward she has earned, and let her works bring her praise at the city gate. (NIV)

Favour is deceitful, and beauty is vain; but a woman that feareth the LORD, she shall be praised. Give her of the fruit of her hands; and let her own works praise her in the gates. (KJV)

Charm is deceptive, and beauty does not last; but a woman who fears the LORD will be greatly praised. Reward her for all she has done. Let her deeds publicly declare her praise. (NLT)

Charm can mislead and beauty soon fades. The woman to be admired and praised is the woman who lives in the Fear-of-God. Give her everything she deserves! Festoon her life with praises! (MSG)

As we complete the study of this woman we find she cares for her household with dignity and grace. She is classy. She has certainly sacrificed and worked hard to maintain her home in the Lord's way. She has sought out bargains to honor the family budget. She prayed over each family member and let go so God could do His work in each, even though it hurt. Is it worth it?

Why are we doing all this? Read *Titus chapter 2 verses 12 and 13* in the Message. *"We're being shown how to turn our backs on a godless, indulgent life, and how to take on a God-filled, God-honoring life. This new life is starting right now, and is whetting our appetites for the glorious day when our great God and Savior, Jesus Christ, appears."*

Becoming the Proverbs 31 woman is a journey, a road traveled with twists and turns and even a few detours. It is not a journey you need to take alone. You are a new woman. *"But whatever I am now, it is all because God poured out his special favor on me – and not without results.. yet it was not I but God who was working through me by his grace." 1Corinthians 15:10 NLT*

You are a beautiful woman, beauty that radiates from inside. *"What matters is not your outer appearance-the styling of your hair, the jewelry you wear, the cut of your clothes-but your inner disposition. Cultivate inner beauty, the gentle, gracious kind that God delights in." I Peter 3:3-4 MSG* With the passage of time you have grown from youthful vanity to honorable womanhood.

God has not put down his yarn yet. He is still stitching you into your life a tapestry of which you are not even aware. You meet people every day and with quiet dignity display the love of the Lord. *Revelation 3:8 "I see what you've done. Now see what I've done. I've opened a door before you that no one can slam shut. You don't have much strength, I know that; you used what you had to keep my Word. You didn't deny me when times were rough.'*

"Show the way for others, and you will find honor in the kingdom." Matthew 5:19 MSG

You are God's word in progress – His masterpiece. You are a woman of great value.

Stitched in Prayer

- PATTERN VERSE: *Revelation 3:8 and Matthew 5:19. "I see what you've done. Now see what I've done. I've opened a door before you that no one can slam shut. You don't have much strength, I know that; you used what you had to keep my Word. You didn't deny me when time were rough." "Show the way for others, and you will find honor in the kingdom."*

- We have now completed the Proverbs 31 woman. How did you grow during this study?

- You are God's masterpiece. How has He revealed this to you in these pages?

- What was your favorite version of Proverbs 31:10-31? Why?

PERSONAL JOURNAL   Today's date: _____

God, be with me during this quiet time. Calm my spirit, help me to focus on you and your love. Open my heart that I may hear you speak to me.

Scripture read today:

During my time with the Lord these people were brought to my mind and I pray for them:

Lord, you have made me mindful of these people. I pray your loving hand on them even if I don't know the situation. I do not need to know that Lord, I only need to follow your Word and pray for them.

For myself Lord I pray you will:

PRAISES

Lord, today I praise you for:

The woman to be admired and praised is the woman who lives in the Fear-of-God
                              Prov. 31:30 The Message

Praise the Lord. Praise God in his sanctuary; praise him in his mighty heavens. Praise him for his acts of power; praise him for his surpassing greatness. Praise him with the sounding of the trumpet, praise him with the harp and lyre, praise him with tambourine and dancing, praise him with the strings and flute, praise him with the clash of cymbals, praise him with resounding cymbals. Let everything that has breath praise the Lord.   Psalm 150

Colors of Salvation Afghan

A Knit and Crochet Bible Study pattern
by TerryAnn Porter

The COLORS OF SALVATION afghan/lapghan

(this version shows errata of the crochet patterns for purple and for blue)

This lesson on various colors representing God's Plan of Salvation is a fun way to learn Scripture and to tell the Salvation story.

Each color is a reminder of God's love and desire to share eternity with us. Salvation is a FREE GIFT, but must be accepted.

Each panel offers a chance to learn a new stitch pattern. I have offered up stitch patterns for a Knit version and for a Crochet version. Both are finished off with crochet edging.

Mix and match the patterns to your liking. Make the panels long enough for an afghan or smaller for a lapghan or child size cover up. (others
have suggested making a tote bag or pillow)

Materials I used and suggest:

Knitting Needles size 9 for Knit version
Crochet Hook "G"or "H" for both versions
Cable hook for Knit version
Yarn needle for both version
1 Skein each color in *Red Heart* or *I Love This Yarn*

- Black
- Orange
- Red
- Gold
- Purple
- Blue
- White
- Green

These are the materials I used. You are welcome to use whatever works best for your tension and skills.

Each panel represents a part of the Salvation story.

Orange represents the fire of hell. We are condemned to life in hell. Romans 6:23 says *"For the wages of sin is death"*. Not the physical death, but the spiritual second death, life eternally separated from God. It is further described in Revelation 21:8 *"But the fearful, and unbelieving, and the abominable, and murderers, and whoremongers, and sorcerers, and idolaters, and all liars, shall have their part in the lake which burns with fire and brimstone, which is a second death"*.

Are you anywhere on that list? *All have sinned and fall short of the glory of God.* Romans 3:23.

White represents the purity of our hearts being washed whiter than snow. We are condemned to death, but because of the blood of Jesus and the sacrifice made, we are made pure. Romans 10:13 says *"For whosoever shall call upon the name of the Lord shall be saved."* That whosoever means YOU. It means me, it means anybody!! All you have to do is call upon Him and trust Him. That cleansing is made possible because *"..the blood of Jesus Christ his Son cleanses us from all sin"* according to 1 John 1:7. *"In the way of righteousness is life; and in the pathway thereof there is no death"* Proverbs 12:28.

When God looks at those who call on Him, he doesn't see the sin, He sees the purity.

Gold is used to represent heaven as described in Revelation 21:18 *"..and the city was pure gold"*. Jesus is preparing a home for you and me. He promises to take us to that home in John 14:2,3 "In my Father's house are many mansions..I am going to prepare a place for you…I will come back and take you to be with me." Your heavenly home is under construction right now.

Blue is the color of the waters of baptism. As a symbol of your commitment to the Lord God you are asked to follow Jesus in baptism. Baptism does not save a person any more than putting on a ring makes your married. You must follow through in the action of commitment. "And he said unto them," in Mark 16: 15,16 "Go into all the world and preach the gospel to every creature. He that believes and is baptized shall be saved". This is the first command given to a believer. Even Jesus was baptized in Luke 3:21.

Green represents growing in Christ. When you first accept Jesus as Lord and Savior, you are like a baby, needing milk and nourishment. But as you grow you learn more of Him and walk in His ways. You grow away from milk and on to meat. You grow in strength. Hebrews 6:1 says *"let us leave the elementary teachings about Christ and go on to maturity"*. Are you growing in Christ?

Purple is the color of royalty. Revelation 11:16 describes Jesus' return saying *"on his robe and on his thigh he has this name written: KING OF KINGS AND LORD OF LORDS"*. Jesus said in Matthew 28:18-20 *"All power is given to me in heaven and in earth. Go and teach all nations, baptizing them in the name of the Father, and of the Son, and of the Holy Ghost and teach them to obey all I have commanded."* With authority we are given our instruction.

But sin separates us from God. That is why the Black which represents sin is used as a divider between each set of panels. Remember Romans 3:23 "for all have sinned and fall short of the glory of God" and Romans 6:23 *"the wages of sin is death."*

That sin has broken the relationship God desires with us.

And that sin can be forgiven. It has been forgiven. Thanks to the Red blood of Jesus. The entire afghan/lapghan is edged in red as a reminder of the price Jesus paid to save you and to save me. That blood was the ransom given for an eternal life with God. Romans 5:8 says *"But God demonstrated his love toward us in this, while we were still sinners, Christ died for us."* God sent His Son to die so you and I could be with Him in heaven. *"For God so loved the world He gave His only Son, that whoever believes in Him will not perish, but have everlasting life*" John 3:16. The key word is "whoever". Anybody. You. Me. "*For Christ died for sins once for all, the righteous for the unrighteous, to bring you to God.*" 1Pet 3:18

Because of the blood shed as a sacrifice, we can live eternally, in heaven with the KING OF KINGS AND LORD OF LORDS.

As you work on this project I pray you will think of the meaning of each color, of the love our Lord has for you and the home being prepared for you. Think about each color and what it represents.

Perhaps you can use the blanket to tell the story of salvation to someone else.

Wrap yourself in the blanket and remember the sacrifice made for you, the ransom price that was paid.

PROJECT NOTES:

The pattern for the Knit version is represented with (K) in the title.
The pattern for the Crochet version is represented with (C) in the title

Idea: make some panels in knit and some in crochet.

On the Knit version, the term "tbl" means "through back loop". This helps reduce curling.
.

ORANGE: GATES OF HELL

Alternate Stitch (C)

With orange, loosely chain 23

Row 1: sc in 2nd ch from hook and in each ch across (22 sc)

Row 2: (right side) ch1, turn; skip first sc (sc,dc) in next sc, *skip next sc, (sc,dc) in next sc; repeat from * across.

Row 3: ch1, turn; (sc,dc) in each dc across.

Repeat Row 3 until desired length is achieved.

Fasten off and weave in ends.

Vertical Weave (K)

NOTE: tbl = through back loop

CO 22

Beginning Border:
Border Row 1: Knit across
Border Row 2: K2, P18, K1, K1tbl

Begin stitch pattern:

Stitch Pattern:
Row 1: (Right Side) K4 *sl 1 as if to Purl, K1, YO, PSSO both the knit st and YO, K2. Repeat
from * across to last 2 stitches, K1, K1tbl

Row 2: K2, P18, K1 K1tbl

Repeat Rows 1 and 2 of stitch pattern until desired length.

Ending Border: same as beginning border

Bind off and weave in ends.

WHITE: PURITY

Half Double Crochet Puffs (C)

White puff of popcorn is the image this pattern brings to my mind. What image do you see?

PUFF STITCH: *YO, insert hook in st indicated, YO and pull up a loop; repeat from * 2 times more. You will now have 7 loops on the hook. YO and draw through all 7 loops.

Loosely chain 23

Row 1: (right side) Work Puff in fifth ch from hook. *ch1, skip next ch, work Puff in next ch.
Repeat from * across

Row 2: Ch 3, turn, work Puff in first ch-1 sp, ch 1 * work Puff in next ch-1 sp, ch 1. Repeat from * across, work Puff in sp of turning ch.

Repeat Row 2 until desired length.

Finish off and weave in ends.

Snowflakes (K)

I love the beauty of freshly fallen snow, pure white, before it is tracked and made dirty by passing traffic.

Note: tbl = through back loop

CO 23

Beginning Border:
Border Row 1: Knit across
Border Row 2: K2, P19, K1, K1tbl

Begin Pattern:
Row 1: (Right Side) K3 *YO, slip 1, K1, PSSO, K1, K2tog, YO, K1. Repeat from *
across to last 2 st. K1, K1tbl

Row 2: K2, P19, K1, K1tbl

Row 3: K4, (YO, K3) across to last 4 st. YO,
K2, K1, K1tbl (29 st now on needle)

Row 4: K2, P25, K1, K1tbl

Row 5: K2, K2tog, YO, slip 1, K1, PSSO, K1,
K2tog *YO, slip 1, K2tog, PSSO, YO, slip 1, K1, PSSO, K1,
K2tog, repeat from * across to
last 4 st, YO, slip1, K1, PSSO, K1, K1tbl (23 st)

Row 6: K2, P19, K1, K1tbl

Row 7: K3 *K2tog, YO, K1, YO, slip1, K1,
PSSO, K1, repeat from * across to last 2 st, K1,
K1tbl

Row 8: K2, P19, K1, K1tbl

Row 9: K4, (YO, K3) across to last 4 st, YO, K3, K1tbl (29 st)

Row 10: K2, P25, K1, K1tbl

Row 11: K3 *K2tog, YO, slip1, K2tog, PSSO, YO, slip1, K1, PSSO, K1, repeat from * across to last 2 st, K1, K1tbl (23 st)

Row 12: K2, P19, K1, K1tbl

Repeat pattern rows 1-12 to desired length.

Ending Border: same as beginning border Bind off and weave in ends.

GOLD: HEAVEN

Crosses (C)
I can't help but think of the cross when I think of heaven

TREBLE STITCH (tr) YO twice, insert hook in st indicated. YO and pull up a loop. You now have 4 loops on the hook. (YO and draw through 2 loops on hook) 3times.

Loosely ch 26

Row 1: (right side) Sc in 2nd ch from hook and in each ch across (25 sc)

Row 2 and 3: ch1, turn, sc across

Row 4: Ch 3 (counts as first dc), turn; dc in next 2 sts. *skip next 2 sts, tr in next 2 sts, working **behind** 2 tr just made, tr in 2 skipped sts, skip next 2 sts, tr in next 2 sts, working in **front** of 2 tr just made, tr in 2 skipped sts, dc in next 3 sts.
Repeat from * across.

Row 5: Repeat Row 4.

For pattern, repeat rows 2-5 until desired length.

Finish off and weave in ends.

Trinity Stitch (K)
The trinity stitch made me think of God the Father, The Son, The Spirit. Three in one like the pattern making 3 stitches in one.

Tbl=through back loop

Loosely cast on 24 stitches.

Beginning Border:
Border Row 1: Knit across
Border Row 2: K2, P20, K1, K1tbl

Begin Pattern:
Row 1: (right side) K2, P20, K1, K1tbl

Row 2: K2 *(K,P,K) all in next st, P3tog, Repeat from * across to last 2 st, K1, K1tbl

Row 3: K2, P20, K1, K1tbl

Row 4: K2, *P3 tog, (K,P,K) all in next st. Repeat from * across to last 2 st, K1, K1tbl.

<u>Repeat rows 1-4</u> until desired length.   Ending Border: Repeat beginning border   Bind off loosely and weave in ends.

BLUE: WATER OF BAPTISM

Lacy V (C)

Loosely ch 26

Row 1: Dc in fifth ch from hook. *skip next 2 ch, (dc,ch 1,dc) in next ch. Repeat from * across.

Row 2: (right side) Ch 3, turn. 2 dc in first ch1 sp, 3 dc in each ch-sp across.

Row 3: Ch 1, turn; sc in first 2 dc. *ch 3, skip next 2dc, sc in next dc. Repeat from * across to last st, sc in top of turning ch.

Row 4: Ch 1, turn. sc in first sc, ch 3, (sc in next ch-3 sp, ch 3) across, skip next sc, sc in last sc.

Row 5: Ch 4, turn; dc in first ch-3 sp, (dc, ch 1, dc) in each ch-3 sp across.

Repeat Rows 2-5 until desired length is achieved. Finish off and weave in ends.

Little Fountain (K)

The stich called "Little Fountain" seemed appropriate for water symbolism

Tbl=through back loop

Loosely cast on 25

Beginning Border:
Border Row 1: Knit across
Border Row 2: K2, P21, K1, K1tbl

Begin Pattern:
Row 1: (RS): K3, *YO, K3, YO, K1. Repeat from * across to last 2 st, K1, K1tbl. (35 st)

Row 2: K2, P31, K1, K1tbl

Row 3: K4, [slip 1 as if to knit, K2tog, PSSO] then [K3, slip 1 as if to knit, K2tog, PSSO] across to last 4 sts, K3, K1tbl   NOTE: repeat
2nd set of [instructions] (25 st)

Row 4: K2, P21, K1, K1tbl

Repeat rows 1-4 until desired length.
Ending Border: Repeat beginning border
Bind off loosely and weave in ends GREEN:

GREEN: GROWING IN CHRIST

Sweet Pea (C)   *Momma always said "eat your peas so you can grow big and strong".*

NOTE: once the border row and first row are completed, you will continue repeating only the row 2 instructions.

ALSO NOTE: Usually you SC or DC *into* the stitch; this patterns call for making your stitch in the space between the stitches, so you will go under the stitch and into the space.

Loosely ch 19

Border row: SC in 2nd ch from hook. SC across (18 st)

Begin Pattern:
Row 1: (right side) Ch 3, turn, DC in same st. *Skip next 2 chs, 5 dc in next next st (this will be called the 5-dc group), skip next 2 sts, dc in next 2 sts (this is a 2-dc group). Repeat from * across to last 3 sts, skip next 2 sts, 3 dc in last st.

Row 2: Ch 1, turn: dc in sp *between* first 2 dc *5 dc in sp *between* dc of next 2-dc group, dc in sp *between* second and third dc of next 5-dc group and in next sp (*between* third and fourth dc). Repeat from * across to last 4 sts, 3 dc in sp *between* last dc and turning ch.

Repeat Row 2 for pattern until desired length is achieved.

Ending border row: ch1, turn, sc across.
Fasten off and weave in ends.

Wheatear (K)

*Wheat grows tall in the fields of the Midwest.
Just as we are to grow tall in Christ.*

NOTE: You will need a cable needle to complete this project

Pattern Stitches:

Cable 4 Back (C4B): slip next 2 sts onto cable needle and hold in back of work, K2 from left needle, K2 from cable needle.

Cable 4 Front (C4F): slip next 2 sts onto cable needle and hold in front of work, K2 from left needle, K2 from cable needle.

Tbl=Through Back Loop

Loosely cast on 29

Beginning Border:
Border Row 1: Knit across
Border Row 2: K2, P25, K1, K1tbl

Pattern:

Row 1: K5, (P8, K3) twice, K1, K1tbl

Row 2: (right side): K2, P1, K1, P1, (C4B, C4F, P1, K1, P1) twice, K1, K1tbl

Row 3: K5, (P8, K3) twice, K1, K1tbl

Row 4: K2, P1, K1, P1, (K8, P1, K1, P1) twice, K1, K1tbl

Repeat Rows 1-4 until desired length.

Ending Border: Repeat beginning border.

Loosely bind off and weave in ends.

PURPLE: ROYALTY

Diamond (C)
I image royalty to have many diamonds, thus this pattern selection for the purple color.

Pattern note: FPtr =
Front Post treble stitch   YO twice. Insert hook from front to back to front going around the post of the stitch indicated (below the are you normally stitch through). YO and draw up a loop. There are now 4 loops on your hook. YO and draw through 2 loops, 3 times.

Loosely ch 26

Row 1: Sc in 2nd ch from hook and in each ch across (25 sc)

Row 2: Ch 1, turn; sc in each sc across

Row 3: Ch 1, turn; sc in each sc across

Row 4: (right side) Ch 1, turn; sc in first 2 sc, work FPtr around first sc on 3rd row below, skip next 4 sc on third row below, work FPtr around next sc on third row below. *Skip next 2 sc from last sc made, sc in next 4sc. Work FPtr around next sc on third row below, skip 4 sc in third row, work FPtr in next sc on third row below. Repeat from * across to last 5 sc, skip next 2 sc from last sc made, sc in last 3 sc.

Row 5: ch 1, turn, sc in each st across

Row 6: ch 1, turn, sc in each st across

Row 7: ch 1, turn, sc in each st across

Row 8: Ch 1, turn; work FPtr around 4th sc on third row below, skip first sc, sc in next 4 sc, *work FPtr around next sc on third row below, skip 4 stitches in the third row down, FPTr around the next stitch on the third row below, skip next 2 sc from last sc made, sc in next 4 sc. Repeat from * across to last 2 sc, work FPtr around next sc on third row below, skip next sc from last sc made, sc in last sc.

Row 9: ch 1, turn, sc in each st across

Row 10: ch 1, turn, sc in each st across

Row 11: ch 1, turn, sc in each st across.

Repeat rows 4-11 for pattern, until desired length is complete.

Finish off and weave in ends.

Diamond Lace (K)

I image royalty to have many diamonds, thus this pattern selection for the purple color.

Tbl=Through Back Loop

Cast on 19 stitches

Beginning Border:
Border Row 1: Knit across
Border Row 2: K2, P15, K1, K1tbl

Begin Pattern:

Row 1:   K6, K2tog, YO, K2, K2tog, YO, K3, YO, SSK, K1, K1tbl

Row 2 and all even rows: :   K2, P15, K1,K1tbl

Row 3:   K5, K2tog, YO, K1, (YO, SSK, K1)twice, K2tog, YO, K2, K1tbl

Row 5:   K4, K2tog, YO, K3, YO, SSK, K1, YO, K3tog, YO, K3, K1tbl

Row 7:   K3, K2tog, YO, K1, YO, SSK, K2, YO, SSK, K2tog, YO, K4, K1tbl

Row 9:   K2, K2tog, YO, K3, YO, SSK, K2, YO, SSK, K5, K1tbl

Row 11: K3, YO, SSK, K1, (K2tog, YO, K1)twice, YO, SSK, K4, K1tbl

Row 13: K4, YO, Sl 1, K2tog, PSSO, YO, K1, K2tog, YO, K3, YO, SSK, K3, K1tbl

Row 15: K5, YO, SSK, K2tog, YO, K2, K2tog, YO, K1, YO, SSK, K2, K1tbl

Row 17: K6, K2tog, YO, K2, K2tog, YO, K3, YO, SSK, K1, K1tbl

Repeat Rows 2-17 for pattern to desired length.

Ending Border: Repeat beginning border.
Bind off and weave in ends.

FINISHING

The same procedure will be used to complete the project whether knit or crochet.

Because sin separates us from God, I have chosen black to separate each panel.

With black yarn, the size G crochet hook and the right side of the panel facing you, attach yarn to the far right corner with a slip stitch. Sc in same stitch. Sc across entire length of panel. (if desired, at end of panel, ch1, turn and sc in each sc across for a 2nd row). Fasten off. Do the same for the other side of the panel. Try to make the same number of sc on each panel.

Place the colors side by side in the order you prefer. I chose Orange, White, Blue, Green, Gold, Purple, but the order is entirely up to you. Think of how you will tell the story of Salvation when deciding on the placement. Using black yarn, stitch panels together.

We are saved by the blood of Jesus. His blood has cleansed us, covered up all our sins. So the entire blanket is edged completely in red.

Once all the panels are attached, weave in ends. Now with right side of blanket facing you, attach Red at any corner on the outside.

Row 1: Ch 1, sc around the entire piece, placing 3sc in each corner, join by slip st into beginning ch.

Row 2: ch1, turn sc in each sc, placing 3sc in each corner, join by slip st into beginning ch.

Row 3: ch3 (counts as 1 dc), turn, dc in next st,* skip next 2 st dc in next 2. Dc in first skipped st, going behind the 2dc you just made, repeat in 2nd skipped st. Repeat from * around. NOTE: at corner do not make the cross over. Dc each 2 or 3 st before and after each corner, making sure to make 3dc in each corner stitch, join by slip st into beginning ch.

Row 4: ch1, turn, sc in each sc, placing 3 sc in each corner, join by slip st into beginning ch.

Row 5: ch1, turn, sc in each sc, placing 3 sc in each corner, join by slip st into beginning ch.

Fasten off. Weave in all ends.

Afterword

Thank you so much for joining me on this journey to discover the Proverbs 31 woman.

If you enjoyed the trip, I would I would like to ask a favor of you. Would you be willing to go back to Amazon and leave a review?

And please, if you find any typos or other errors contact me directly. Even though this has been reviewed by numerous eyes with many edits, little things sometimes tend to slip through. Think of it as a dropped stitch you didn't find until your recipient unwrapped the crocheted shawl you made (yes, that has happened to me). You may email me at TerryAnn@KnittingBibleStudy.com

Printed by Amazon Italia Logistica S.r.l.
Torrazza Piemonte (TO), Italy

49625111R00057